TORNADO

TORNADO

CHRISTOPHER LAMPTON

THE MILLBROOK PRESS
BROOKFIELD, CT
A DISASTER! BOOK

Cover photograph courtesy of Superstock

Illustrations by Pat Scully

Photographs courtesy of Superstock: pp. 6, 10–11, 16–17;
Turner Entertainment Company: p. 8; NCAR: pp. 9, 21, 24, 25,
29 (all), 30, 38; National Weather Service: pp. 12, 33, 36, 46,
49, 54 (© Mark Besh, Bill Bishop, 1978); Wide World Photos, Inc.:
p. 18; © Howard Bluestein, Science Source/Photo Researchers:
p. 31; *The Raleigh News and Observer*, Jennifer Steib: pp. 34–
35; National Severe Storms Laboratory: pp. 41, 42, 45, 47.

Cataloging-in-Publication Data
Lampton, Christopher
Tornado / by Christopher Lampton
p.   cm.—(A Disaster! Book)
Bibliography p.   Includes index.
Summary: The terror of tornadoes unfolds with this
account of the most devastating natural phenomenon
in the world. Includes several precautions.
ISBN 1-56294-032-5

ISBN 0-395-63644-2 (pbk.)

1. Tornadoes. 2. Cyclones. 3. Meteorology. 4. Winds.
I. Title. II. Series.
551.5   1991

123456789 - WO - 96 95 94 93 92

CONTENTS

TORNADOES AREN'T FUN!

It's one of the most frightening, awesome sights in the world. Few people get to see it in person. Most of us, however, have seen photographs or films of it—if only in the movie *The Wizard of Oz*. A black, funnel-shaped cloud drops down out of the sky. It tears across the surface of the earth, turning houses and buildings into broken bits of wood and brick.

It is a tornado. For its size, it is the most devastating natural phenomenon in the world.

Usually, it begins as an ordinary thunderstorm. Dark clouds fill the sky. Torrential rains sweep the land. Sharp gusts of wind scatter leaves and slam doors.

Lightning crackles across the heavens. Peals of thunder echo with every flash. The lightning comes faster and faster. It seems as if the lightning and thunder are almost nonstop.

Then, above the sound of the thunder, comes another roar. The sound is like that of a freight train rumbling down a narrow

Above: lightning crackles across the heavens in the kinds of storms that can produce tornadoes. In fact, lightning is one of the most common weather phenomena. It strikes earth about 100 times every second. Opposite: a tornado picks up Dorothy's house and drops it in the fictional land of Oz in the classic movie The Wizard of Oz.

tunnel. It becomes almost deafening. Then you see it—the dark funnel looming overhead!

You run into your basement seeking shelter. Perhaps you crawl under an old sofa for protection. From upstairs, you hear the clunking and rattling of flying debris over the roar of the storm. It seems as if you wait hours for the storm to pass. Yet it is really only a few

minutes. Finally, as the noise of the storm dies away, you steel your nerves and crawl reluctantly out of the basement—to find that the rest of your house is no longer there. The wooden walls are scattered about in the yard. All your possessions are strewn about among them. Plumbing fixtures stick straight up out of the ground, no longer attached to anything. Broken glass lies all around.

Tornadoes can wreck one house completely while leaving others nearby totally undamaged.

You gather up your strength and start picking up your collection of videotapes and audio cassettes. Then you hear another roar. You look up. The funnel cloud is coming back at you again!

You dive back into the basement and take shelter under the sofa yet another time. Tornadoes aren't a lot of fun.

No sight is more frightening than that of the dark, funnel-shaped cloud of a tornado heading your way.

TORNADOES: WHEN AND WHERE

Tornadoes can happen anywhere in the world. Most of them, however, happen in the American Midwest, along a strip known as "Tornado Alley." This strip runs from Texas and Kansas in the south to Canada in the north. But tornadoes sometimes occur elsewhere in the United States and in other parts of the world as well.

Although tornadoes can strike at any time of the year, most of them happen in spring and fall. And spring tornadoes are probably more common than the fall kind. May is the biggest month for tornadoes. December and January are when the fewest tornadoes happen.

Tornadoes are short-lived storms. They often last no more than minutes. But those few minutes can be terrifying indeed. Sometimes, tornadoes come in packs, with one storm spawning multiple tornadoes. Each of these can cause damage if it touches down in the right place.

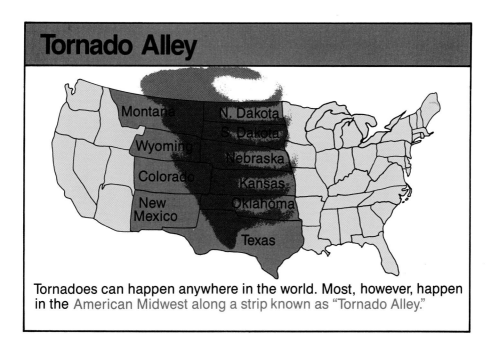

Tornado Alley

Montana

N. Dakota

Wyoming

S. Dakota

Nebraska

Colorado

Kansas

New Mexico

Oklahoma

Texas

Tornadoes can happen anywhere in the world. Most, however, happen in the American Midwest along a strip known as "Tornado Alley."

In 1965, for instance, a storm known as the Palm Sunday Outbreak wreaked havoc across Ohio and five neighboring states. Over a period of nine hours, 37 tornadoes appeared and disappeared. They caused destruction wherever they went. One wrecked a shopping center and 100 homes. Another tore down two churches and several houses. Yet another tossed a farmhouse 60 feet into the air. A total of 271 people were killed by the storm.

Forty years earlier, in 1925, the deadliest tornado in U.S. history ripped across the American Midwest. Known as the Tri-State Tornado, it first appeared in southeast Missouri at one o'clock in the afternoon. It proceeded to destroy the entire town of Annapolis. It

then cut across Illinois, leveling one town after another. Finally, it veered into Indiana.

The tornado lasted for three and a half hours. This is a long time for a single tornado. During its existence, it killed 695 people.

Tornado damage in Minnesota from the Palm Sunday Outbreak of 1965.

It destroyed four towns completely, damaged six others, and demolished 15,000 homes. No tornado before or since has been as deadly. Worse, the same storm spawned two more tornadoes that took 100 lives between them.

A tornado demolishes a school in Huntsville, Alabama, in 1989.

In the so-called Super Outbreak of 1974, tornadoes roared across 13 different states in the American Southeast over a period of two days. This is an area not commonly hit by tornadoes. More than 300 people were killed and 28,000 houses destroyed. Fortunately, weather forecasters were able to give storm warnings in advance. Thus, many people had time to prepare for the onslaught. But the storms were still quite devastating. This was especially so because basements and storm shelters (which can provide some protection against such storms) are relatively rare in the Southeast.

More than seventy tornadoes slashed through seven states on April 26, 1991, killing at least thirty people. States affected were Kansas, Texas, Oklahoma, Arkansas, Missouri, Nebraska, and Iowa. Kansas was especially hard hit. One mobile park, for example, was completely demolished. Two hundred and ninety trailers were ruined, and pieces of metal from the park were found 17 miles away.

No, tornadoes aren't a lot of fun.

THE MAKING OF A TORNADO

Scientists who study weather are called *meteorologists*. Meteorologists don't fully understand what makes a tornado happen. But they do know one thing for sure: Tornadoes occur during thunderstorms. And thunderstorms happen when air is rising very quickly.

Why does air rise? There are several reasons. Sometimes, air rises when it blows over a mountain. The air has to "climb" the mountain in order to get over it, just as you would. This is called *orographic lifting* of air.

Sometimes, air is blowing from two or more different directions. When it comes together in the middle, it is forced upward. This is called *convergence* of air.

Mostly, though, air rises when it is warm. The tiny particles that make up the air, called *molecules,* become excited when they are heated. This causes them to move apart. The air becomes thinner and lighter. It is forced upward by the heavier air around it, like bubbles rising in boiling water.

*The base of cumulonimbus
(thunderhead) clouds over a field.*

Orographic Lifting of Air

Air has to "climb" a mountain in order to get over it, just as you would. This is called orographic lifting of air.

Air Climbing Over the Mountains

On a hot summer day, the sun heats the ground. The ground, in turn, heats the air. (The sun never heats the air directly.) The air becomes warm and starts to rise. As it rises, it carries water with it, in the form of a gas called *water vapor*.

Where does this water vapor come from? It enters the air when the air passes over water. Hot molecules of water jump out of the water and into the air. There they remain as a gas. As the air rises, it carries this water with it.

But as air rises, it gets colder. (This is why snow often forms on mountaintops, even though it may be spring or summer. The air on the mountaintop is almost always colder than the air near the mountain's base.) As the air gets colder, the warm molecules of

Convergence of Air

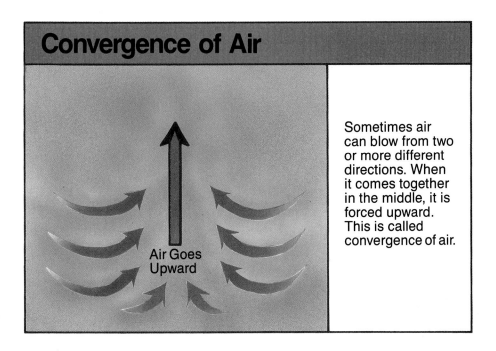

Air Goes Upward

Sometimes air can blow from two or more different directions. When it comes together in the middle, it is forced upward. This is called convergence of air.

water vapor cool off. They turn back into tiny droplets of liquid water. These droplets, floating suspended in the air, become a *cloud.*

The warmer the air is, the more water vapor it can hold. On especially hot days, the warm rising air can form towering clouds with thick white columns. Meteorologists call these *cumulonimbus clouds*. We often refer to them as *thunderheads*.

Water droplets floating in the air can sometimes bump together to form bigger droplets. These fall out of the cloud to become rain. Thunderheads have an unusually large amount of water in them. Thus, they can produce especially thick and intense rains of the type we call *thunderstorms*.

And thunderstorms can sometimes produce tornadoes.

Left: altocumulus castellanus clouds high in the sky. Above: cumulonimbus clouds produce driving rainstorms that can last from one to several hours. Depending on the temperature of the surrounding air, either rain or hail falls to the ground.

FROM OUT OF
THE STORM

Why do some thunderstorms produce tornadoes though most do not? That's hard to say. Meteorologists believe that tornadoes are most common in areas where a layer of cold, dry air flows over the top of a layer of warm, wet air. These conditions are most often found in the American Midwest, which is why most tornadoes occur there.

Under these conditions, the air becomes highly *unstable*. This is a term meteorologists use to describe conditions under which air is very likely to rise. When air rises, it carries water upward with it. This, in turn, can cause storms. Thus, unstable air conditions often lead to storms.

As air rises, the *air pressure* goes down. Air pressure is the force with which air presses down on the ground below. Thus, we say that the area where the air is rising is a *low-pressure area*.

To replace the air that is rising in the low-pressure area, air comes rushing in from all sides. As we saw earlier, when air con-

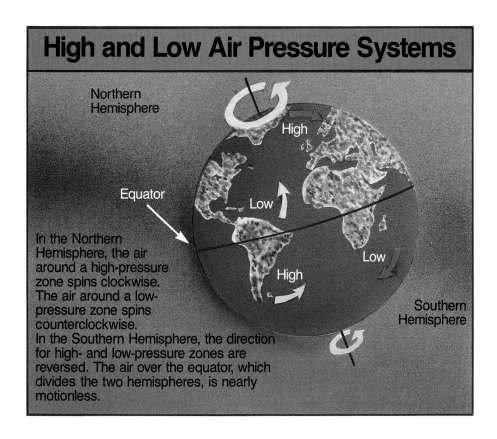

High and Low Air Pressure Systems

Northern
Hemisphere

High

Equator

Low

Low

High

Southern
Hemisphere

In the Northern
Hemisphere, the air
around a high-pressure
zone spins clockwise.
The air around a low-
pressure zone spins
counterclockwise.
In the Southern Hemisphere, the direction
for high- and low-pressure zones are
reversed. The air over the equator, which
divides the two hemispheres, is nearly
motionless.

verges—comes together from all sides—it pushes still more air up-ward. This raises still more water vapor up into the clouds.

Under certain conditions, the rotation of the earth can influence what happens. It can give a spin to a thin column of rising air. To see an example of this rotation, just look at the water as it drains out of your bathtub. Instead of going straight down the drain, the water spirals downward in a counterclockwise direction. When a thin column of rising air starts rotating very quickly like this, it can become a tornado. (It is possible that this rotation is helped along by masses of air moving in opposite directions. These air masses rub up against one another. The friction between the air masses can start the air spinning very rapidly.)

The tornado begins in the clouds high above the ground. A cone or cylinder of spinning air, called a *funnel cloud,* forms. This funnel can grow until it actually touches the ground and becomes a tornado. Fortunately, it rarely remains on the ground for more than a few minutes. Then it lifts back into the clouds again. But during those few minutes, the tornado can cause terrible destruction. This is especially true if the tornado touches the ground in a heavily populated area.

The winds in a tornado are extremely fast. Even the weakest tornado can produce winds of more than 75 miles per hour (mph). And scientists believe that the most powerful tornadoes have wind speeds of close to 350 mph. These may be the fastest natural winds on earth. We can't measure these wind speeds directly, however. The winds destroy the instruments that are used to measure their speed. Instead, wind speed is estimated by examining the damage the winds cause. Films of tornadoes in action are also studied.

In the Northern Hemisphere, the tornado winds usually rotate in a counterclockwise direction. This is because of the twist they are given by the spinning of the earth. In the Southern Hemisphere, they rotate in a clockwise direction. There they are given the opposite spin by the earth. Most tornadoes, however, occur in the Northern Hemisphere. Thus, most tornadoes spin counterclockwise. Meteorologists refer to the counterclockwise rotation of air as *cyclonic rotation,* and tornadoes are sometimes also referred to as *cyclones.* This last term, however, is generally reserved for larger storms such as hurricanes. A more common term for tornado is "twister."

This spectacular sequence of pictures shows a tornado forming over Colorado on June 6, 1990, touching the ground, then lifting back up into the clouds.

When tornadoes touch the ground, they stir up leaves and dust and anything else that is loose. These particles give the tornado a brownish or black color.

Although tornadoes are made up of nothing more than air, they are not invisible the way air normally is. When they touch the ground, they suck up particles of dust and anything else that may be lying around loose. This can include leaves and blades of grass. As these particles swirl around in the tornado, they give it a dark color, usually black or dark brown. Tornadoes that touch down on colored soil or clay can take on other colors as well.

Tornadoes that move over water actually suck water up into their whirling winds. They change color in the process. Such a waterborne tornado is called a *waterspout*. The winds in a waterspout move more slowly than the winds in a regular tornado. Thus, these storms are less deadly than land-based storms.

A waterspout over the tropics.

DESTRUCTIVE EFFECTS OF TORNADOES

Until recently, meteorologists believed that the most destructive thing about a tornado was the drop in air pressure that went with it. The air in the middle of a tornado presses down with only about 90 percent of the force of normal air. At one time, scientists thought that this drop in air pressure actually caused houses and buildings to explode. The idea was that the pressure inside the house would become greater than the pressure outside the house. The air inside the house would then tear the structure apart as it tried to escape, like air bursting from a popped balloon.

This is no longer believed to happen. The drop in air pressure inside a tornado, however, is still strong enough to cause windowpanes to blow out.

Meteorologists now believe that the most destructive thing about tornadoes are the powerful winds that they produce. These winds can blow down buildings. They can lift automobiles off the ground and hurl them through the air.

The most destructive thing about tornadoes is the winds they produce. This house lost its entire top floor and all the westward-facing doors and windows, thanks to the winds of a tornado.

Wind pressing against an object, such as a building, gains force with the speed of the wind. You might think, for instance, that a 300-mph wind would have four times the force of a 75-mph wind.

Steel beams bowed by tornado winds in Raleigh, North Carolina.

This isn't true. Actually, it has 16 times the force of a 75-mph wind! Since tornado winds can blow at speeds of up to 350 mph, they can be powerful indeed!

*A mobile home is not a safe place
to be when a tornado strikes.*

Winds that blow with that much force can do great damage to anything that gets in their way. Pieces of straw have been driven right through solid wood. Chickens have been completely stripped of their feathers. People, cows, and even cars have been lifted into the air and tossed great distances.

And yet tornado winds can be surprisingly unpredictable. One person's house might be blown down completely while the next-door neighbor's house might be left untouched. Babies have been carried off by the wind, only to be dropped unhurt several blocks away. The top floors of some three-story buildings have been sheared off by tornadoes while the ground floors have remained completely intact.

Tornadoes move along with the thunderstorms that spawn them. Some tornadoes loop back and forth as they move. Thus, it's possible for a tornado to pass over the same place twice, from two different directions.

The speed of a tornado's winds actually varies according to which side of the tornado you're on. Why? The movement of the *whole* tornado adds extra speed to some of the winds *within* the tornado. Because the tornado is rotating counterclockwise, the winds on the right-hand side of the tornado (as viewed from behind the tornado) are moving in the same direction in which the tornado is traveling. This means that the actual speed of the tornado winds on the right-hand side is the speed of the tornado's rotation *plus* the speed at which the entire storm is moving. To the people and houses in the path of the tornado, the winds on the right-hand side of a tornado can seem to be moving as much as 150 mph faster than the winds on the left-hand side! So if you ever get caught in a tornado, try to stay to its left!

INSIDE A
TORNADO

It's not easy to study tornadoes. They are both relatively rare and very destructive. Most instruments used for studying normal weather are useless for studying a tornado. The winds rip them apart. Special instruments can be designed for studying tornadoes. But if they are simply placed out in the middle of a field in the hope that a tornado will come along, they will probably never get a chance to do their job.

Perhaps the ideal situation would be for a meteorologist and his or her instruments to be picked up off the ground by a tornado and then be deposited safely in the middle of a field 15 minutes later. But this would be very risky, and no one should try it.

Still, people have actually been caught up in tornadoes and lived to tell about it. One of the most famous such incidents occurred in 1928 in Kansas. A farmer named Will Keller found himself directly beneath a tornado. He was able to look up into the middle of the twister for quite a few seconds. Although he was not a meteorologist, he later wrote a description of his experience that has since become famous.

"At long last the great shaggy end of the funnel hung directly overhead," Keller wrote. "Everything was as still as death. There was a strong gassy odor, and it seemed that I could not breathe. There was a screaming, hissing sound coming directly from the end of the funnel. I looked up and to my astonishment I saw right up into the heart of the tornado. There was a circular opening in the center of the funnel, about fifty or one hundred feet in diameter, and extending straight upward for a distance of at least one half-mile, as best as I could judge under the circumstances. The walls of this opening were of rotating clouds and the whole was made brilliantly visible by constant flashes of lightning which zigzagged from side to side. Had it not been for the lightning I could not have seen the opening, not any distance up into it anyway.

"Around the lower rim of the great vortex small tornadoes were constantly forming and breaking away. These looked like tails as they writhed their way around the end of the funnel. It was these that made the hissing noise. . . .

"The opening was entirely hollow except for something which I could not exactly make out, but suppose that it was a detached wind cloud. This thing was in the center and was moving up and down. . . ." [Quoted in Ralph Hardy, *et al., The Weather Book,* Boston: Little, Brown and Company, 1982.]

When Keller says that he could not breathe, that's probably because of the drop in air pressure inside the tornado. This would make the air around him thinner than the air he was used to breathing. The lightning flashes inside the tornado are also a well-known weather event. Tornadoes produce almost constant lightning. Much of it occurs inside the funnel cloud itself.

When viewed at night, tornadoes often seem to glow a dull yellow. This is due to the lightning flashing inside.

But meteorologists want to be able to see inside a tornado for themselves. Thus, at the National Oceanographic and Atmospheric Administration (NOAA), a portable package of instruments has been built that scientists call the "totable tornado observatory"—TOTO, for short. (The shortened name was no doubt inspired by Dorothy's dog in *The Wizard of Oz,* who gets carried "over the rainbow" by a tornado.)

When a tornado is believed to be on the way, a pair of NOAA meteorologists toss TOTO into the back of a truck. They then drive straight into the twister's path. They drop TOTO off and hightail it back to safety as quickly as they can. With luck, the tornado will pass right over the top of TOTO and TOTO will be able to take instrument readings. Assuming TOTO survives the storm (as it is designed to do), the readings can be retrieved later.

TOTO, the mobile observatory
used by NOAA to study tornadoes.

WATCHING FOR TORNADOES

In Kansas City, Missouri, meteorologists at the National Severe Storms Forecast Center keep a constant watch for signs of tornado weather. They look at pictures from satellites high above the earth. They also study photographs from weather radar installations and data collected by instruments in balloons. They use this information to determine if a tornado is likely to happen anywhere in North America.

Tornadoes occur only when there are special weather conditions. The air pressure must be falling. The wind is usually coming from the south or southeast. And the humidity is high, indicating lots of water vapor in the air. Thunderstorms are usually present. (The presence of a thunderstorm doesn't mean that there's going to be a tornado, however. In fact, only a very small number of thunderstorms ever produce tornadoes. Most thunderstorms come and go with little, if any, damage.)

This weather balloon contains a radiosonde, a miniature radio transmitter that sends back information to meteorologists on air temperature, pressure, and humidity levels.

Meteorologists at the National Severe Storms Fore-
cast Center in Kansas City, Missouri, look for signs
of developing tornadoes and severe thunderstorms.

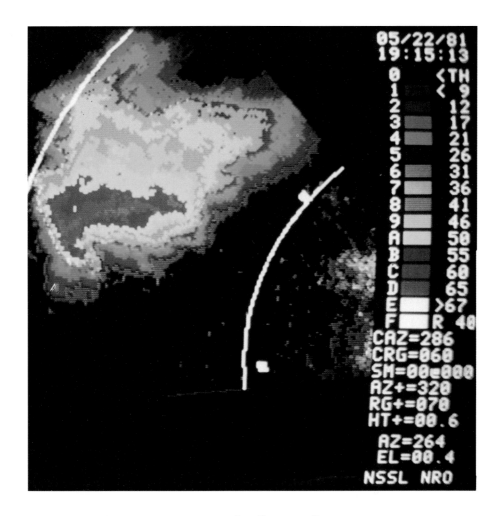

This Doppler radar screen at the Severe Storms
Laboratory in Norman, Oklahoma, shows a tornado
in action. The colors on the computer screen are
coded for showing wind speeds and direction. Red
represents the fastest speed away from the radar.
Yellow represents the fastest speed toward the radar.

When these conditions exist, the Severe Storms Forecast Center contacts the National Weather Service. And the National Weather Service issues a *tornado watch*. This doesn't mean that anybody has seen a tornado yet. It just means that conditions are ripe for a tornado to form. If you hear that a tornado watch has been issued, don't get too worried. A tornado is still unlikely. And, even if there is one, it's not likely to touch down where you are. Still, you might want to keep your eyes open for suspicious-looking funnel clouds.

What if a funnel cloud has actually been sighted? Or what if weather radar shows the weather patterns that usually precede the formation of a funnel cloud? Then a *tornado warning* is issued. This means that a tornado is very likely in the immediate area for which the warning is given. If you are in that area, you should immediately take precautions against a tornado. We'll discuss some of those precautions in the next section.

What signs should you look for if you hear that a tornado might be on the way? One sign, obviously, is a thunderstorm. Tornadoes generally accompany thunderstorms. Thus, rain and thunder may indicate that a tornado is forming. The vast majority of thunderstorms, however, don't have tornadoes associated with them, so you still shouldn't get too worried.

The most telling sign of a tornado is the well-known funnel cloud. But not all funnel-shaped clouds are tornadoes. It's not uncommon for a column of dark cloud to form underneath a thunderhead. Most such columns are not tornadoes. If the column is rotating, however, it may mean trouble.

If it's dark outside or raining heavily, you may not be able to see the funnel cloud at all. Fortunately, tornadoes also make a lot of noise. When a tornado touches the ground, it makes a sound

The funnel shown here is not that of a tornado. It is blowing dust combined with a particularly low-lying shelf of clouds.

that has been described as a loud roaring. This roaring might re-semble the sound made by a runaway freight train, a hive of giant bees, or a jet taking off. And the constant lightning inside the funnel cloud produces constant thunder. The tornado should be loud enough for you to hear easily. In fact, the sound will be almost deafening for many miles around!

WHAT TO DO WHEN A TORNADO IS COMING

So, there's been a tornado warning issued for your area. You think a tornado's really on the way. What should you do?

Well, one thing that you should *not* do is go outdoors, except briefly in order to reach a safer shelter. Most people who die in a tornado are killed by flying debris. A pane of glass, for instance, hurled through the air at tornado wind speeds can chop a living creature in two. Other flying objects can be just as deadly. Seek shelter from the storm *indoors*. There should be a solid wall between you and the flying debris.

Don't take shelter inside an automobile, though. Your car can be lifted right off the ground by the storm. Or the car windows can be shattered, spraying debris throughout the inside of the vehicle.

If you find yourself in a car when the storm hits, open the windows a little rather than close them. That way they can't be shattered by the drop in air pressure. And trying to outrace the storm in a car really isn't a very good idea. The path of a tornado is unpredictable. You might find yourself heading right into it instead of away from it! If there's a ditch by the side of the road, park the car, get out, and run to the ditch. But don't go downwind from the car, because it might be blown into the ditch with you.

Once indoors, stay away from windows. A basement is the safest place inside the house. If you don't have a basement, stay on the ground floor and get under a heavy piece of furniture such as a bed or a table. There you'll be protected from flying glass and falling objects. Most tornadoes come from the southeast. Therefore, you are better off in the north part of the house, away from the winds.

One fairly safe place to be in a tornado is in a *storm cellar.* These are underground shelters that have been built in some yards in the Midwest. They are completely separate from the houses and are places where people can hide from the storm. Because no flying debris at all can penetrate these shelters, they are very safe in a tornado. But few houses have storm cellars, especially outside of the American Midwest.

If you're in a public place, find out if there are public shelters available. Many buildings have basements, some of which have been set aside as shelter areas. If you know where the basement is, go there right away. Otherwise, ask a police officer where shelter is available.

Don't go into large rooms, such as school cafeterias, with long roofs or skylights that may be exposed directly to the tornado. The roof could collapse—and then you'd be almost as bad off as if you were outside! And avoid rooms with entrances or large windows facing to the south or east. In fact, avoid windows altogether.

Where to Go in Case of A Tornado

NO

Do not go outdoors.

Stay out of cars. If you are in a car when a tornado hits, open your windows a few inches.

Do not stay in large rooms, such as a school cafeteria. Long roofs and large panels of glass can be dangerous.

YES

Make sure a solid wall is between you and the outdoors.

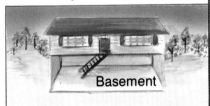

One of the best places to be is in a basement. If a basement is nearby go there right away.

If there is no basement nearby, stay under a large piece of furniture on the north side of the house.

A totally enclosed, small space such as a closet or bath-
room in the north part of a house is the safest place to
stay if you don't have a basement. The National Weather
Service created this cartoon character to illustrate safety
procedures that should be followed in case of a tornado.

If you live in a trailer or a mobile home, consider finding shelter somewhere else. Trailers have actually been lifted into the air and carried away by a tornado.

Wherever you go, take a battery-operated radio with you. That way, you can listen to official weather advisories. Also, keep your head covered so that you won't be hit by flying debris.

Most important of all, don't panic! When disaster strikes, it always pays to keep calm. The chances that the tornado will come straight at you are slim. Just follow the rules outlined above and wait out the storm. Perhaps the best thing about a tornado is that it's over with very quickly!

BUILDING A STORM CELLAR

You may never have need for a storm cellar. A basement is actually the safest place in a tornado, so if you have one, use it! But if you live in an area where tornadoes happen frequently and you don't have a basement but you do have a large yard, your family might consider building a storm cellar. It could save your life someday.

Like all cellars, a storm cellar goes underground, in a large hole in the earth. Once the hole is solidly roofed over, the earth itself will provide shelter against the fury of the tornado. Most important, the storm cellar will protect you from flying debris during the tornado.

For this reason, it's important to build the storm cellar far from your house. Although debris from the house probably won't be able to get inside the shelter, it could keep you from getting back out. A brick wall falling on top of the storm cellar could be disastrous.

The storm cellar doesn't need to be especially big, since you won't be staying in it for a long time. It should be tall enough to stand in or at least to sit in comfortably. And there should be room for all of your family members, pets, and a couple of friends besides.

What should the storm cellar be made out of? Concrete walls will make the shelter sturdy and strong, but wood will do. Cinder blocks and bricks are also suitable materials for walls. A wooden roof covered with a thick layer of dirt will keep debris from entering the shelter. And a hinged wooden door that opens down into the cellar will let you in and out.

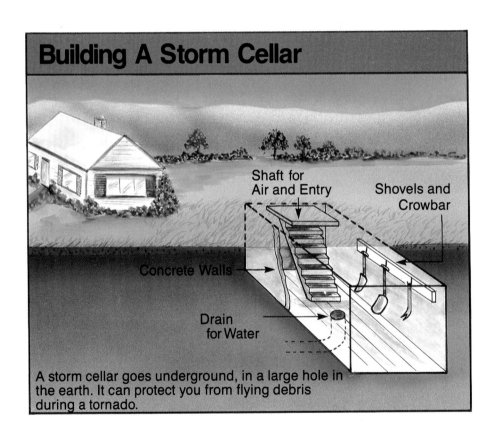

Building A Storm Cellar

Shaft for Air and Entry

Shovels and Crowbar

Concrete Walls

Drain for Water

A storm cellar goes underground, in a large hole in the earth. It can protect you from flying debris during a tornado.

There should be some way to drain water out of the shelter, so that it won't flood when it rains. (You don't want to get caught inside the storm cellar during a tornado only to find it filling up with water all around you!) If no other drain is available, you can dig a hole in the floor into the earth below to serve as a well.

Ventilation is also important. You'll need to be able to breathe. A shaft leading from the cellar up to the surface will let air into the cellar. It can also be used to get out of the cellar if the door should become blocked during the storm.

You may want to keep emergency supplies in the shelter. Food probably isn't necessary, because you won't be in the cellar long enough to get hungry. But you may want to keep some digging tools and a crowbar around, in case you have to unblock the exit. Check the tools often to make sure they aren't getting rusty.

Even if you never need the storm cellar, it's nice to know that it's there. A tornado is a frightening event, but it's a lot less frightening if you're prepared for it.

GLOSSARY

air pressure—the pressure, or weight, with which air presses down on the ground below it.

cloud—a collection of water droplets suspended in the air.

convergence—when air comes together from two or more different directions, forcing the air to rise.

cumulonimbus cloud—a large, towering cloud created by rapidly rising moist air; commonly produces thunderstorms and is better known as a *thunderhead*.

cyclone—the name sometimes used for tornadoes, because they rotate in a cyclonic motion.

cyclonic rotation—the rotation of air in a counterclockwise direction.

funnel cloud—the cylindrical or funnel-shaped cloud that is the most obvious sign of a tornado.

low-pressure area—an area where the air presses down on the ground with less weight than normal.

meteorologist—a scientist who studies the weather.

molecules—the tiny particles of which air and most other substances are made; molecules are, in turn, made up of atoms.

orographic lifting—when air is lifted as it passes over an object such as a mountain.

storm cellar—an underground shelter built to protect people in severe storms and from the destruction caused by tornadoes.

thunderhead—the common name for a cumulonimbus cloud.

thunderstorm—a violent rainstorm accompanied by lightning.

tornado warning—an official announcement that a tornado has been spotted in the immediate area.

tornado watch—an official announcement that conditions are ripe for a tornado.

unstable air—air that tends to rise.

water vapor—the gas form of water, commonly found as part of the air around you.

waterspout—a tornado over water.

RECOMMENDED READING

Armbruster, Ann, and Elizabeth A. Taylor. *Tornadoes.* New York: Franklin Watts, 1989.

Erickson, John. *Violent Storms.* Blue Ridge Summit, Pa.: Tab Books, 1988.

Gibilisi, Stan. *Violent Weather: Hurricanes, Tornadoes, and Storms.* Blue Ridge Summit, Pa.: Tab Books, 1984.

Lambert, David, and Ralph Hardy. *Weather and Its Work.* New York: Facts on File Publications, 1984.

Pettigrew, Mark. *Weather.* New York: Gloucester Press, 1987.

Webster, Vera. *Weather Experiments.* Chicago: Children's Press, 1982.

INDEX